THE SECOND COMING OF

CHRIST

BY

HENRY CLAY MORRISON

First Fruits Press
Wilmore, Kentucky
c2013

ISBN: 9781621711353 (Print), 9781621711360 (Digital)

The Second Coming of Christ by Henry Clay Morrison
First Fruits Press, © 2013
Previously published by the Pentecostal Publishing Company, c1914

Digital version at
http://place.asburyseminary.edu/firstfruitsheritagematerial/27/

Morrison, H. C. (Henry Clay), 1857-1942.
    The second coming of Christ / by Henry Clay Morrison.
    120 p. ; 21 cm.
    Wilmore, Ky. : First Fruits Press, c2013.
    Reprint. Previously published: Louisville, Ky. : Pentecostal Pub. Co.,
    c1914.
    ISBN: 9781621711353 (pbk.)
    1. Second Advent. I. Title.
    BT885 .M65 2013   232.6

Cover Design by Haley Hill

asburyseminary.edu
800.2ASBURY
204 North Lexington Avenue
Wilmore, Kentucky 40390

First Fruits
THE ACADEMIC OPEN PRESS OF ASBURY SEMINARY

The Second Coming of Christ.

By

Rev. H. C. Morrison, D. D

Author of

"The Baptism with the Holy Ghost," "From the
Pulpit to Perdition," "World Tonr of Evangelism," "Life Sketches and Sermons," "Thoughts
For the Thoughtful," "The Confessions
of a Backslider," "The Two Law-
yers," "Open Letters to the
Church," etc.

PUBLISHED BY
THE PENTECOSTAL PUBLISHING COMPANY,
LOUISVILLE, KY.

CONTENTS.

CONTENTS

This little volume is dedicated to
"The Holiness People,"
and all other Christian people who
trust alone in Jesus Christ for salvation from all sin.

PREFACE.

In writing this book it has been the least of our thought to undertake anything like a full discussion of the subject under consideration. The book is written to awaken interest in the precious doctrine it holds forth and suggest a further study of the subject as contained in the Scriptures and in many excellent and more exhaustive publications on the same theme.

There are many phases of the subject we have not discussed at all. The book, as we send it forth, is the outgrowth and enlargement of a sermon we have preached on many occasions under which we have seen profound conviction, numbers of sinners converted, believers sanctified, and the Lord's people greatly edified and blessed. We send it forth earnestly praying that God may make it a blessing to those who read its pages.

Faithfully yours in service and watching,
H. C. MORRISON.

"Watch therefore, for ye know neither the day nor the hour wherein the Son of man cometh."—Jesus, Matt. 25:13.

CHAPTER I.

THE BUDDING FIG TREE.

If Jesus Christ had have come into the world the first time as He will come the second time, the world would have been utterly unprepared to receive Him. When God appeared in clouds of smoke on Mt. Sinai, the people "did exceedingly fear and quake." When Jesus appears in the clouds, coming the second time in His glory, those who have rejected Him and are without the white robes of His righteousness, will call for rocks and mountains to fall upon them and hide them from the "face of Him that sitteth upon the throne."

In the redemption of the race and restoration of all things, it was necessary that our Lord should come twice into the world. First, to die for its redemption and inaugurate the gospel plan of salvation. Second, to set up His kingdom on earth

and reign in triumph and blessedness over
His redeemed people.

All through His ministry Christ called
attention to the fact that He would come
again into the world. His parables, sermons and sayings abound in gracious
promises of His coming and in exhortations
to His followers to be prepared for that
glorious event. On the last solemn evening
He spent with His disciples before His
crucifixion, He comforted their sad hearts
with the following gracious promise: "I
go to prepare a place for you.   And if I
go and prepare a place for you, I will
come again, and receive you unto myself;
that where I am, there ye may be also."
St. John 14:2, 3.

His many references to His second coming awakened in His disciples a profound
interest and a keen desire to know the time
when He would return.   The date of His
coming He never gave them, but on the
other hand assured them that the time was

the secret of the Father and that, not knowing the hour, it behooved them to be always
ready. He did, however, give them certain signs that would indicate to them the
nearness of His appearing.

In Matt. 24:32, 33, He says: "Now
learn a parable of the fig tree; when his
branch is yet tender, and putteth forth
leaves, ye know that the summer is nigh:
So likewise ye, when ye shall see all these
things, know that it is near, even at the
doors." From this scripture we learn that
while the day of the coming of the Lord is
not given, there are certain events that must
take place, and certain conditions that will
exist just prior to the conclusion of the gospel dispensation,, and these signs are
as positive evidence that the coming of Christ draweth nigh, as the
bursting of the buds of springtime are
indicative of the approach of summer. The
blind man cannot see the buds swelling on
the bough under the warm influence of the

sunshine and shower, nevertheless, the buds are easily discerned by those who have eyes to see.

It is not to be supposed that men who do not believe in Christ, do not love Him, and do not desire Him, would be able to discern the signs of His coming. There are those who do believe in Him, but whose eyes are blinded by ecclesiastical ambition, prejudice or false teaching so that they are unable to discern the signs of the times. These signs will be visible only to those who watch for them with the eagerness and longing that arise from the passionate love of a bride, who awaits with joyful expectation the coming of her bridegroom.

Among devout Christians who believe that Jesus Christ will return in triumph to claim His bride, there are two schools of teaching: The post-millennial, and the pre-millennial. Post-millennialists believe that the preaching of the gospel will so powerfully influence society that gradually the

world will be converted, evil will be overcome, and the millennium—a thousand
years of universal peace and blessedness—
will come upon the earth; and that at the
end of this thousand years the Lord Jesus
Christ will appear in great glory and power to inaugurate the judgment, catch away
His bride into heaven, and drive the wicked into outer darkness.

Pre-millennialists believe that the gospel
must be preached to all the world for a witness, that by many it will be rejected, that
wicked men will wax worse and worse;
that Christ's coming will be as in the days
of Noah, when the world is not expecting
or desiring Him; and while vast multitudes
are living in rebellion and sin, that just as
Noah gathered the few righteous persons
into the ark, so the Lord Jesus will gather
His redeemed bride to the place prepared
for them, and then, as the flood destroyed
the wicked in the days of Noah, so great
tribulation will come upon the earth; that

later on Jesus will appear with His people, set up His kingdom, bind and cast Satan into the pit and reign in great glory for a thousand years.

We believe that the Scriptures abundantly prove the pre-millennial doctrine to be true, and we believe that conditions in the world today and the outlook for human history is quite in accord with the teachings of the Word of God as believed by pre-millennialists.

Among devout and earnest Christians in all lands there is a very marked and deep conviction that we are rapidly approaching the end, not of the world, but of the age, of this dispensation. The flood marked the end of a dispensation, and the beginning of a new and better one. The fall of Jerusalem and breaking up of the Israelitish nation marked the end of a dispensation and the introduction of a better one; the coming of the Lord Jesus Christ will mark the end of this dispensation, and the introduction of a far better one in which the kingdoms of this world will become the kingdoms of our Lord and His Christ.

That there have been fanatical teachings on this subject there is no doubt, but such teachings do not at all invalidate the teachings of Jesus Christ and His apostles on the subject; neither should mistakes of Christians in the past intimidate or hinder Christians of the present from "comforting one another with these words," of hope and consolation.

Men who have fixed dates for the coming of the Lord have always gone contrary to the plain teachings of Jesus Christ. He has distinctly said: "No man knoweth the day nor the hour wherein the Son of man cometh." But He has given signs that indicate the nearness of the time when He will appear, and it is quite reasonable to suppose that those who love Him and long for His appearing should be watching for those signs.

"For the time will come when they will not endure sound doctrine; but after their own lusts shall they heap to themselves teachers, having itching ears. And they shall turn away their ears from the truth, and shall be turned unto fables." 2 Tim. 4:3, 4.

CHAPTER II.

THE APOSTASY.

We believe the signs of the times unmis-
takably indicate that the coming of the
Lord Jesus is much nearer than most people suppose it to be. It is our purpose in
this treatise, to examine some present conditions and see if there are not swelling
buds on the fig tree of prophecy to thrill
the devoted heart with the hope that the
return of the Lord is near. First, we wish
to call attention to the great apostasy pre-
dicted in the New Testament scriptures.
To the Thessalonians Paul says, "Let no
man deceive you by any means; for that
day shall not come, except there come a
falling away first." II. Thes. 2:3.

The above scripture is taken from a discussion concerning the coming of our Lord.
The Apostle Paul also writes the follow-

17

ing to Timothy: "Now the Spirit speaketh expressly, that in the latter times some shall depart from the faith, giving heed to seducing spirits, and doctrines of devils." I. Tim. 4:1.

In his second letter to Timothy Paul says, "For the time will come when they will not endure sound doctrine; but after their own lusts shall they heap to themselves teachers, having itching ears; And they shall turn away their ears from the truth, and shall be turned unto fables." II. Tim. 4:3, 4. The conditions described in these scriptures are to exist just before the coming of our Lord; and it seems to us there can be no reasonable doubt that these conditions do exist today in a marked and startling degree.

We are well aware that backslidings, apostasies, and dark days have come to the church through the past centuries, but today we have conditions of unbelief, false doctrines and deceptive philosophies destroying the souls of men which have scarcely been paralleled in the history of the church. Those oriental countries where the gospel was first preached have sadly become a vast moral waste. Southern Europe, in which the great Apostle labored, and where the religion of Jesus Christ secured a footing and made rapid headway in the early history of this dispensation, has fallen into an apostasy sad to contemplate. France, Italy and Spain, though dotted over with churches, and burdened with priests, offer at the same time one of the most needy, and one of the most difficult mission fields in all the world. The decadence of genuine spirituality, the dead formalism, and degrading superstitions of these great countries are appalling. Germany is blighted with destructive criticism. German scholars in spiritual blindness have torn the inspired Scriptures to tatters, and the State Church has become a system of dead forms and ceremonies denying the power of godliness

In the British Isles the drift is toward Romanism, and everywhere there are evidences of a fearful state of spiritual decadence, while the destructive criticism in the church and the blatant infidelity of the streets march shoulder to shoulder to overthrow the influence of the Bible and aggressive evangelism, destroying the faith and hardening the hearts of the people.

In these United States the whole trend in morals and religion is alarming in the extreme. Our great universities are becoming powerful centers for the cultivation of unbelief in, and ridicule of the sacred Scriptures. Many prominent pulpits deny the inspiration of much of the Bible, and openly disclaim any faith in a number of the great fundamental doctrines of divine truth. Thousands of our Protestant ministers are unsettled in their faith and in fact, are quite at sea with reference to the

authenticity and authority of Holy Writ;
while the rising tide of popular unbelief
is breaking away the barriers of the old
faith and flooding the land with a reckless
and blasphemous infidelity.

The skeptical teachings in the colleges,
the taint of unbelief and ridicule in litera-
ture, and the uncertain sound in the pulpit,
are digging the foundations from beneath
the faith of the people, and countless
multitudes and millions of human beings in
the streets of our populous cities utterly disregard God, the Bible, the Sabbath day,
the Church, and all of the authority and
restraints of the divine law.

We cannot overlook the fact that in the
midst of these untoward conditions, all
manner of false teaching is springing up
and finding ready reception among the
drifting masses. Note the tremendous
growth of Eddyism, the magnificent tem-
ples being erected all over the land into
which multitudes crowd to read Mrs. Ed-

dy's unscientific and unscriptural scribblings. New Theology, New Thought, all sorts of ancient heathen religions, and modern spiritualism attract the attention, beguile and destroy the souls of the people.

The growth and audacity of Romanism, with its infallible pope, its superstitious juggleries over the bones of the saints, and its masses, with its huge financial graft attachment, of prayers for the dead, and powerful political influence, are enough to alarm every sober-thinking citizen of our nation. One of the most alarming features of the situation is the fact that the great masses of our church membership, supposed to be somewhat orthodox, have come to believe that sin is an essential part of human nature, that holiness is an impossibility, that the Word of God cannot be intelligently understood, that His commandments cannot be obeyed, that the atonement is not sufficient to reach and overcome the depravity and proneness of the human heart to evil. Under these false teachings and misconceptions of divine truth, and the provisions made in the sufferings of Christ for the redemption of men, all hungering and thirsting after righteousness and desire for holiness are being quenched out of the soul of believers, the people are drifting into lukewarmness, backsliding and falling under the domination of the world, the flesh, and the devil.

Because of these conditions, it has come to pass that in thousands of great congregations of professed Christians, it would be almost an insult to the people for the preacher of the gospel to stand in the pulpit, explain and enforce the plain teachings of the Word of God, which point out the sufficiency of the atonement, the renewing power of regeneration, the cleansing power of sanctification, and the glorious possibilities and absolute necessity of a holy heart and a righteous life.

We firmly believe that the dusk of the
great apostasy is upon us, and that it will
deepen into a darkness of spiritual decadence and death fearful to contemplate.
God's laws are violated, His Son is rejected, and crucified afresh, the Holy Spirit is ridiculed and grieved, while a great
Niagara of lost souls is pouring into the
abyss of eternal night.

We are not unmindful of the devout
ministers, faithful people, earnest evangelists and great missionary movements in
the world today; but just now we are
calling attention to the great apostasy, the
unbelief and wickedness that are sweeping
the earth like a cyclone of moral ruin.

This very general apostasy and the
widespread influence of skeptical teaching
and worldliness is recognized and lamented
everywhere, not only by thoughtful and devout people in the church, but among sober
and thinking men in the world generally.
In books, pamphlets, magazine articles, and

the daily press we find a general lamenta-
tion among thoughtful and observant men
in all walks and conditions of life over the
dearth of real Christian devotion and the
tremendous aggressiveness of the evil
forces; there is a widespread and general
fear in the mind and hearts of men with reference to the immediate future of the race.
It seems as if the foundations of society are
shaking beneath us. There is unrest, dis-
satisfaction, and fearful forebodings in the
minds of the people that are undoubtedly
the forerunners of one of the greatest catas-
trophes and most remarkable and radical
changes in all the history of the world.

Many sincere people believe that the ca-
lamities, volcanic eruptions, earthquakes,
and destructive floods are the voice of
warning from a compassionate God who is
striving to call the attention of the people
to the frailty and uncertainty of the things
of this life and to make immediate preparation for the tremendous events which are

marching rapidly toward the culmination of the centuries.

Scientific physicians will tell you that sin has so polluted the the physical life, so shattered the nervous system, and sown broadcast disease of every kind that millions of people are unfit to wed and produce children.   Immorality is making such inroads upon society that state legislatures are passing laws to prevent the marriage of those persons whose physical condition is such that their offspring must necessarily be fearfully diseased; and the most learned and thoughtful men are telling us that something radical must be done, and done soon, or the world will be crowded with hospitals and lunatic asylums; that the fearful and increasing number of suicides will multiply, and finally the human race will become extinct.

Once before in the history of man he became so wicked and polluted that he was unfit to inhabit the earth and propagate the species, and God swept the earth with the flood; "Whereby the world that then was, being overflowed with water, perished: But the heavens and the earth, which are now, by the same word are kept in store, reserved unto fire against the day of Judgment and perdition of ungodly men." 2 Peter 3:6, 7.

"Let your loins be girded about, and your lights burning; And ye yourselves like unto men that wait for their Lord, when He will return from the wedding; that when He cometh and knocketh, they may open unto Him immediately. Blessed are those servants, whom the Lord when He cometh shall find watching."—Jesus, Luke 12:25-27.

CHAPTER III.

THE GOSPEL NOT A FAILURE.

We have failed to find in the Scriptures a single passage indicating that the gospel dispensation will wind up in a triumphant conquest of the world for righteousness. We find the Scriptures everywhere teaching the reverse of this, and this is no evidence that the gospel scheme is a failure.

There is no coersion in the gospel. God nowhere proposes to force men into righteousness, submission to His law or acceptance of His truth; He always and everywhere recognizes their free agency. It was never intended that the gospel should save the men who reject it. It is no argument against a medicine, that it does not heal men who refuse to take it, or food, that it does not nourish men who refuse to eat it; or the gospel that it does not save

29

men who stubbornly and persistently refuse to receive it and trust in its saving power.

Our post-millennium brethren insist that their premillennial brethren discount the power of Christ to save, and make the gospel dispensation a failure, if it does not finally result in the conversion of the entire population of the earth. Has not many a postmillennial preacher gone into town, village or community and preached the gospel long, faithfully and earnestly and seen only a very small part of the population converted, while the vast majority of the people not only disregard his warning, exhortation and invitations to salvation in Christ but actually became harder of heart and more wicked because of their attitude of resistance against his message of mercy, adding to their sin of violation of divine law, another and perhaps greater sin, the rejection of divine mercy.

In leaving such a community does the faithful preacher conclude that the gospel is a failure? By no means so. The gospel has graciously saved those who have accepted it; to them it has the power of eternal truth to deliver from guilt and sin, and to prepare them to meet their coming Lord in peace. Those who have rejected the gospel have failed and must perish. Nevertheless, the gospel has been offered to them and will appear as a witness against them, and in that great day they will be judged in the light of the mercy and truth which they spurned.

The Lord Jesus does not say that when all the world has been converted and saved, then the end shall come, but He does say, "And this gospel of the kingdom shall be preached in all the world for a witness unto all nations; and then shall the end come." Matt. 24:14.

It is well understood that the dispensation before the flood ended in destruction. Does any intelligent man say that God and His truth were a failure in the antediluvian age? By no means so. All thoughtful, pious men say that the people of that age were wicked and rebellious, that they rejected warning and mercy, and having done so, there was nothing left for them but destruction.

The Hebrew dispensation closed out with the fall of Jerusalem and the carrying away of the Jews into captivity. Will any honest may say that God failed, that His revelation, prophets, and plans were insufficient to accomplish His gracious purposes? Certainly not. The people trampled on His truth, persecuted and murdered His prophets and His Son, utterly refused to fall into harmony with His plans, and brought upon themselves destruction.

When the present dispensation comes to a close in the binding of Satan, the overthrow of his power in the world, the destruction of those who have rejected Christ, and the coming of our Lord in glory to set up His kingdom on the earth, no man, intelligent or ignorant, devout or otherwise, will say that the gospel of Jesus Christ has been a failure. They will say it was, and is eternal truth, and a glorious success to those who received it, but that it had no power to save those who rejected it. "Whosoever shall fall upon this stone shall be broken; but on whomsoever it shall fall, it will grind him to powder." Luke 20:18.

It must be borne in mind that the gospel dispensation is a period of probation; that man is a free agent; that for the present the wheat and tares are growing together; that Satan is at large roaming the earth seeking whom he may devour, and that legions of evil spirits and wicked people under his dominion are helping to tempt and destroy multitudes of human beings. This condition of things is not to last; it is in the mind of God a temporary, fixed period. Satan's career on this globe will come to an end; he has great wrath because he knows that he hath but a short time.

When the wicked spirits said to Jesus: "Why hast thou come to torment us before our time?" they knew that they had an appointed time to remain in this world, and then to be driven out of it and be confined to their place in the pit, and they knew that their time had not yet come. Jesus Christ recognized this fact and did not send them into their final place of abode.

It was the will and wisdom of God in the development of character and bringing men into a state of holiness which is to stand the tests of eternity, to place him in a world of temptation fraught with trials and temptations, to give him the gospel, the merits of a crucified Savior, the powerful influences, leadings, and inspirations of the Holy Spirit, the church with the ministry, and the various means of grace for his salvation, upbuilding, and perfecting; and after the gospel has been preached in all the world for a witness, giving men an opportunity to be saved, He will bring this dispensation to a close. Satan and his minions will be driven out of this world, those who rejected Jesus will be driven out with him, and Jesus will set up His kingdom and all those glorious prophecies concerning the triumph of the kingdom of God in the world, when, "the knowledge of the glory of the Lord shall cover the earth as the waters cover the sea," and, "the kingdoms of this world are become the kingdoms of our Lord and His Christ" shall be fulfilled.

This was the thought in the mind of our Savior, when He put His disciples and His church to praying, "Thy kingdom come, thy will be done in earth as the angels do it in heaven." This prayer will be answered when Christ appears with His resurrected and translated saints. Satan, demons, sinners, and rejecters of Christ and His truth, will be driven away, and Jesus Christ will reign and rule in supreme and undisputed authority.

This talk about "the gospel being a failure," if everybody is not converted during this dispensation, is a pitiful begging of the question. If that be true, it has already been a failure; vast millions of people have rejected it and died in their sins and will continue so to do.   It was never intended that the gospel should force men into a state of obedience and devotion; it offers to give salvation, and if that offer is rejected, the rejecter must bear the consequences.

Jesus says: "Behold, I stand at the door and knock," but He never breaks the door down.   The time is coming, and coming soon, when those who have spurned the authority of God, violated His laws, rejected His Son, grieved His Spirit, and given themselves over to the dominion and control of the devil will be crying for rocks and mountains to fall on them and hide them from the face of the Lord coming in the clouds of glory.   Then we shall hear no more talk of the gospel being a failure.

The preaching of destructive criticism,

uncertainty and doubt, notions and opin-
ions of men, instead of God's message,
the skeptical teaching in colleges and litera-
ture, the unbelief, worldliness and wickedness which is the inevitable harvest of such
sowing, the growth and rampant spirit of
Romanism, Mormonism, Eddyism, Rus-
sellism, with the disregard of law, and the
common decencies of life, are rapidly preparing the way for perilous times.

"This know also, that in the last days perilous times shall come. For men shall be lovers of their own selves, covetous, boasters, proud, blasphemers, disobedient to parents, unthankful, unholy, without natural affection, trucebreakers, false accusers, incontinent, fierce, despisers of those that are good, heady, highminded lovers of pleasure more than lovers of God; having a form of godliness, but denying the power thereof: from such turn away." 2 Timothy 3:1-5.

CHAPTER IV.

PERILOUS TIMES.

The Scriptures foretell a fearful state of society at the close of the gospel dispensation. These conditions will be the logical consequences of the rejection of the truth and salvation offered in Christ. The widespread rejection of the Bible, the authority of God, the deity of Jesus, the personality and leadership of the Holy Spirit, are now opening wide the flood-gates of sin for the inflow of all forms of evil.

Paul, writing to Timothy, says: "This know also, that in the last days perilous times shall come. For men shall be lovers of their own selves, covetous, boasters, proud, blasphemers, disobedient to parents, unthankful, unholy, without natural affection, trucebreakers, false accusers, incontinent, fierce, despisers of those that are

good, high-minded, lovers of pleasures
more than lovers of God, having a form of
godliness, but denying the power thereof."
II. Tim. 3:1-5.

We are not able to understand how our
postmillennial brethren can reconcile their
views with these teachings of the Scriptures.   Undoubtedly, this prophecy of St.
Paul is now being fulfilled before our eyes.
Whatever we have had in the past, whatever the future may hold for us, there can
be no question but that we are now living
in perilous times.   Restlessness and uneasi-
ness in human society is widespread
throughout the world.

There is much talk of peace but war
and bloodshed, with all their attendant evils
prevail, and while millions of human beings suffer for necessary food and the people stagger beneath a load of taxation,
the nations in hot haste spend multi-
plied millions of money in preparation for
the destruction of human life.

Note this saying of the Apostles: "Men shall be lovers of their own selves, covetous." How fully this scripture is fulfilled in the great, greedy trusts of the country. Are men today saying, "Give us this day our daily bread?" Nay, verily! They are not asking God to give them anything; they are boldly taking everything in sight.

One great trust corners all the wheat and breadstuffs; another corners the fabrics for clothing; another corners building material; another corners the meat supply. The vast herds of cattle are fat and must be butchered because it is ready for the market, and would be expensive to keep on the hoof, but the great trusts, in order to keep up the exorbitant prices of meat, kill and freeze hundreds of thousands of fat carcasses in cold storage, until the price of beef is so high that a poor man cannot buy a juicy steak to put milk into the flabby breasts of his hard-worked and starving wife, that she may furnish nourishment for

the emaciated and diseased baby that per-
ishes in her bony arms for lack of sufficient
food.

Another corporation controls dairy products, another corners poultry products,
another the dried fruit, another the fresh
fruit, another controls the oil, another the output of coal; and so
it comes to pass that God's earth, with its
rich resources and supplies for the needs of
mankind, is so controlled and manipulated
by human selfishness that vast millions of
people live in misery, and die prematurely
because of the lack of proper nourishment,
housing and clothing, and go up to bear
witness before God of the mismanagement,
starvation, and slaughter that are going on
in this fallen and sinful world.

The Apostle tells Timothy that men
will be "boasters, proud, blasphemers, disobedient to parents, unthankful and unholy." These fearful conditions have
reached to so high a tide in the earth that

no man can move among its masses without being constantly reminded, if he will only stop to think, that the conditions herein specified, exist in an alarming degree among his fellowbeings. The people "sit down to eat and drink, and rise up to play." Holiness is a subject for ridicule among church members; multitudes of preachers in their pulpits oppose that holiness which comes to a human soul through the cleansing blood of Jesus Christ.

"Unnatural affection!" Think of the war being waged today in our society against the coming of innocent babes into the home. The physicians tell us that the slaughter of the unborn is widespread, and newspapers reveal the fact that infanticide among our civilized people is quite common. Meanwhile, the fondness of poodle dogs grows into a shocking passion. It is reported that babies can be bought in some of our great cities at two dollars a piece, while poodle dogs are eagerly sought in

the market at prices ranging from a hundred dollars and upward. *Unnatural affection* indeed!

If Jesus should come in the clouds of glory today, and those who are not expecting Him should complain that He appeared without proper notification, He could easily point them to this famous quotation from Paul to Timothy and assert that every prediction contained in it, is fulfilled in present day conditions.

What thoughtful man is not impressed with the adulterations and dishonesty in commerce, the trickery and selfishness in politics, the stupid ignorance and brutality of the whiskey traffic, the prostitution, lewdness and general spirit of lawlessness which prevails throughout the earth, constanly fostered with the growth of unbelief in God and His eternal truth. Time would fail us to tell of the outrage and crimes committed under the sun; the oppression by the rich, the despair and vindictiveness of the poor, and the rising tide of perilous times.

The men who have the intellectual capacity and financial ability to manipulate conditions so as to bring plenty and happiness to the race, in stupid selfishness seek to secure incalculable wealth, while humanity suffers the untold evil consequences. While thousands of people shiver with cold, millions of cords of wood rot in the forest; while tens of thousands of lean, bony-fingered little children in our great cities never had a whole peach, pear or orange in their dirty little hands through all of their wretched lives, tons on tons of God's golden fruit rot upon the ground. While earth's bounties are heaped away in elevators and cold storage, lean-faced fathers and mothers look at each other with sad eyes over scantily supplied tables.

Meanwhile, the spirit of unrest grows and the demon of vengeance crouches to leap upon its fat and unexpected victim.

Perilous times have come, but we have only seen the scouting parties, the mere advance guard of the onmarching army of wickedness, rebellion and anarchy, the logical outcome of the rejection of Jesus and His gospel, and the choosing of Satan and rallying beneath his black banner for the awful day of destruction.

The antediluvians sinned, rejected warnings, refused to repent and finally met their doom when the mad waves of the deluge lashed in fury the highest mountain peaks. The Hebrew people killed the prophets, crucified Jesus Christ and met their doom when the Roman hosts pressed in upon Jerusalem from every side, until starved with famine, enshrouded with fire, and choked with blood, their sacred city fell into the hands of their heathen conquerors and, carried into captivity, they were sold into slavery throughout the pagan markets of the world.

The gospel dispensation has been characterized with backslidings, rejections, unbeliefs, selfishness and sin. In many countries where the faith once flourished, now superstition hangs like a black pall. Our highest civilizations are filling the coffers of their governments with the blood money of the whiskey traffic, and we have in the incubator of social conditions the eggs which will hatch the vipers to sting society with the poison of unbelief and lawlessness that will sweep the earth with great tribulation. We have sown to the wind, and we must reap the whirlwind.

The advance guard of "perilous times" is upon us and the heavy columns of fearful days of destruction and high tide of human sorrow are marching forward with unhalting and rapid tread.

"Behold, the days come, saith the Lord, that I will raise up unto David a righteous Branch, and a King shall reign and prosper, and shall execute judgment and justice in the earth. In His days Judah shall be saved and Israel shall dwell safely; and this is His name whereby He shall be called, *The Lord our Righteousness.*"   Jeremiah 23:5-8.

Chapter V.

RETURN OF THE JEWS.

The prophetical scriptures clearly teach that the Jewish people will be gathered again into the Holy Land. This gathering will undoubtedly take place before the coming of Christ. The general belief of premillennial Bible students is that the appearing of the Lord will occur very soon after the restoration of the Jews to Palestine.

We will quote a few passages of Scripture from the prophets in proof of the teaching that the Jews will return to the Holy Land: "For, lo, the day is come, saith the Lord, that I will bring again the captivity of my people Israel and Judah, saith the Lord: and I will cause them to return to the land which I gave to their fathers, and they shall possess it." Jer. 30:3.

In the 10th and 11th verses of this same chapter we read the following: "Therefore fear thou not, O my servant Jacob, saith the Lord; neither be dismayed, O Israel: for, lo, I will save thee from afar and thy seed from the land of their captivity: and Jacob shall return, and shall be in rest, and be quiet, and none shall make him afraid. For I am with thee, saith the Lord, to save thee: though I make a full end of all nations whither I have scattered thee, yet will I not make a full end of thee: I will correct thee in a measure, and will not leave thee altogether unpunished."

This prophecy evidently does not refer to any of the gatherings of the Hebrew people to Palestine in the past, but refers to that far more general and final gathering of the Hebrew people to their own country shortly before the appearing of our Lord.

In Lamentations 4:22, we read, "The punishment of thine iniquity is accomplished, O daughter of Zion: he will no more carry thee away into captivity." Perhaps no one of the ancient prophets has so much to say of this final restoration of the Hebrews as the prophet Ezekiel. He speaks with great ecstasy of the restoration of the land, and rebuilding of the waste places. Note the following: "But ye, O mountains of Israel, ye shall shoot forth your branches, and yield your fruit to my people of Israel; for they are at hand to come. For, behold, I am for you and I will turn unto you, and ye shall be tilled and sown: and I will multiply men upon you, all the house of Israel, even all of it: and the city shall be inhabited and the wastes shall be builded: and I will multiply upon man and beast; and they shall increase and bring fruit: and I will settle you after your old estates, and will do better unto you than at your beginning:

and ye shall know that I am the Lord,"
Ezk. 36:8-11.

In the same chapter from which the
above is taken, we read from the 23rd and
24th verses, "And I will sanctify my great
name which was profaned among the
heathen, which ye have profaned in the
midst of them: and the heathen shall know
that I am the Lord, saith the Lord God,
when I shall be sanctified in you before
their eyes, for I shall take you from among
the heathen, and gather you out of all
countries and will bring you into your own
land." These scriptures are very clear.
It is the purpose of God in the restoration
of the Hebrews, in exact fulfillment of
these ancient prophecies to prove to the
heathen, the destructive critics, the church,
and whole world, that the Holy Scriptures
are inspired; that He is a covenant-keeping
God; that what He has promised He will
bring to pass.

Continuing in this same chapter from

verse 33 to 36, we read the reiteration and
confirmation of the above promises: "Thus
saith the Lord God: in the day that I shall
have cleansed you from all your iniquities
I shall also cause you to dwell in the cities,
and the wastes shall be builded. And the
desolate land shall be tilled, whereas it lay
desolate in the sight of all that passed by.
And they shall say, this land that was desolate is become like the garden of Eden;
and the waste and desolate and ruined cities are become fenced and are inhabited.
Then the heathen that are left round about
you shall know that I the Lord build the
ruined places, and plant that that was desolate: I the Lord have spoken it, and I will
do it."

One of the very interesting features with
regard to these splendid prophecies is the
fact that they are now being actually fulfilled. The Jews are rapidly returning
to the Holy Land. There are some 60,-
000 of them now living in Jerusalem, and

many prosperous colonies are springing up in Palestine. A few years ago, while traveling in that country, my eyes were gladdened as I beheld with delight, that history is dove-tailing into prophecy and Palestine is being restored. I was especially impressed while walking arour about Jerusalem with the prophecy contained in Jer. 31:38, 39. "Behold, the day is come, saith the Lord, that the city shall be builded to the Lord from the tower of Hananeel unto the gate of the corner. And the measuring line shall yet go forth over against it upon the hill Gareb, and shall compass about to Goath."

While in Jerusalem, I asked a friend who has resided there for a number of years, with reference to this prophecy, and he walked with me to the hill Gareb, saying to me as we went along, that the "measuring line had already gone forth." When we arrived there we found the slope of the hillside covered with a beautiful new village and occupied by 1,300 Jews who had recently returned there from foreign countries, and had gone into their new homes before the carpenters had time to complete them, and some of the gables had been temporarily closed in with corrugated iron. We also saw a new village being hurried to completion in the outskirts of Joppa, with houses sufficient to accommodate a thousand Jews who were coming to them just as soon as they could be completed.

I called the attention of my traveling companion to the fact that while many of our modern scholars are ridiculing the Holy Scriptures, that these prophecies concerning the return of the Jews are being most wonderfully fulfilled before our eyes; and we rejoiced together, as we realized that our faith in the eternal truth of God's word rests upon an unshaken foundation. The Lord says of this restoration and rebuilding, "It shall not be plucked up, nor thrown down any more for ever."

That this restoration of the Jews is to be very general, will be seen from the following scriptures: "Therefore thus saith the Lord God; now will I bring again the captivity of Jacob, and have mercy upon the whole house of Israel, and will be jealous for my holy name; after that they have borne their shame, and all their trespasses whereby they have trespassed against me, when they have dwelt safely in their land, and none made them afraid. When I have brought them again from the people, and gathered them out of their enemies' lands, and am sanctified in them in the sight of many nations; then shall they know that I am the Lord their God which caused them to be led into captivity among the heathen: but I have gathered them unto their own land, and have left none of them any more there. Neither will I hide my face any more from them: for I have poured out my Spirit upon the house of Israel saith the Lord God." Ezk. 39:25-29.

We are aware that some people try to give these prophecies some sort of a spiritual interpretation, trying to make it appear that they refer to a period of great grace and blessing in the history of the Christian Church. It would hardly seem worth while to try to argue with or convince such people. The prophecies that the Israelites should be scattered into all the world, have been actually and literally fulfilled. The prophecies of their restoration will be as literally fulfilled as those referring to their scattering have been.

We will close these quotations with reference to the restoration of Israel with a beautiful selection from Jeremiah 16:14-16. "Therefore, behold, the day is come, saith the Lord, that it shall no more be said, the Lord liveth, that brought up the children of Israel out of the land of Egypt; but, the Lord liveth, that brought up the children of Israel from the land of the north, and from all the land whither He had driven them: and I will bring them again into their land that I gave unto their fathers. Behold, I will send for many fishers, saith the Lord, and they shall fish them; and I will send for many hunters, and they shall hunt them from every mountain, and from every hill, and out of all the holes of the rocks."

"Therefore, behold, the days come, saith the Lord, that it shall no more be said, The Lord liveth, that brought up the children of Israel out of the land of Egypt; But, The Lord liveth, that brought up the children of Israel from the land of the north, and from all the lands whither He had driven them; and I will bring them again into their land that I gave unto their fathers. Behold, I will send for many fishers, saith the Lord, and they shall fish them; and after will I send for many hunters, and they shall hunt them from every mountain, and from every hill ,and out of the holes of the rocks." Jer. 16:14-16.

CHAPTER VI.

THE RETURN OF THE JEWS.

(*Continued.*)

Just as the Old Testament Scriptures were shut up in the Hebrew language and the New Testament Scriptures were shut up in the Greek language, so Palestine has been shut up in the grip and under the tyrannical rule of a nonprogressive people, and in this way through the centuries, it has been preserved in its topography and customs, just as it was in the days of Christ and the apostles; a powerful external witness of the inspiration of the scriptures. The traveler who visits Palestine on landing in that country realizes that he has stepped back into conditions and scenes, customs and habits as they existed two thousand years ago. It was the will of God that the country should thus be preserved as a powerful corroborating witness of the sayings of Jesus and the writings of the apostles.

It is said that during one of his campaigns, King William, the grandfather of the present Emperor of Germany, sitting about his camp fire, said to his chaplain, "Chaplain, what is the best external evidence of the inspiration of the Bible? Answer me not in argument or process of reasoning, but briefly—in a word." The chaplain answered, "Sire—The Jews." "Ha!" said King William, "That is splendid. You could not have given me a better answer. The Jews, as they exist today, are a remarkable fulfillment of prophecy, and a powerful witness to the inspiration of the Bible."

Jerusalem is to be trodden down by the Gentiles until the time of the Gentiles be ended   There is every reason to believe that the waning power of the "unspeakable Turk" over Palestine will soon be broken.

When the hand of destiny marks the hour on the dial plate of time, it must be so. We rest our faith in God and wait patiently.

When Palestine comes from under the iron yoke of Turkey, then no doubt, "The time of the Gentiles" will have ceased. The Jews who are now settling up and improving the country are the advance guard of divine purpose preparing the land to receive the multitudes which will then begin to flow into it. Again its fruitful hills will wave with luxuriant orchards of olives, figs, oranges and pomegranates. Again the mountain sides will be turned into great vineyards of most delicious grapes, and the valleys will be golden with ripening grain, and the goodly land will with milk and honey flow, and the Jews, who through all their wanderings and sufferings during two thousand years, have under God, preserved their Hebrew blood as pure and untainted as that which flowed in the veins of Moses and David, will come flocking home from all the lands in which they have been scattered, like doves to their windows, and the inspired promises of God will have triumphed over the unbeliefs of men.

That the Jews are rapidly returning there can be no doubt. Unbelievers, however, attribute these facts to various causes and put prophecy and all divine guidance entirely out of the matter. Of course unbelievers do not propose to be convinced.

Mr. Nathan Straus, one of the most wealthy and influential Jews in the United States, has retired from business and proposes to devote the remainder of his life and a very large part of his fortune to the improvement of the city of Jerusalem. Mr. Straus has been a man of great public spirit in this country and has spent some millions of dollars in various public charities. He has been especially interested in the pasteurizing of milk for the prevention of tuberculosis. He has also done some charitable work in Jerusalem. He now proposes to establish a pure water supply in Jerusalem which will cost about $500,-000.

Mr. Straus was recently in the Holy Land, and on return said to a newspaper man: "You know I am non-denominational, although I believe that no preacher of the gospel of any denomination should undertake to convey a great spiritual message to any sect without first experiencing the extraordinary religious sensibility which a visit to Palestine will give him. It is a wonderful experience, a necessary part of his education, to immerse himself in the remarkable atmosphere of religious feeling which pervades the Holy Land."

This would indicate that Mr. Straus is not only a man of great wealth and business capacity, but a man of genuine spiritual sensibilities. Of course, we all know that a man may be a most earnest, excellent, and fruitful preacher without ever

seeing Jerusalem, yet no man has had the
privilege of visiting that country who
would not be impressed with these sayings
of this great Jew.   It *is* a remarkable thing
to "immerse" oneself in the religious atmosphere that pervades the Holy Land,
especially Jerusalem.

Mr. Straus says: "The needs of Palestine are very great.   I have done all
that a man of my means can afford, but
it is only a mite to what could be accomplished if sufficient funds were available.
Whoever comes forward and supplies the
means will be instrumental in creating a
resurrected Holy Land again flowing with
milk and honey.   I went to Jerusalem
last year because I was drawn there by
associations of the Holy Land; I found
conditions that appalled me.   Starvation
and disease held the people in their grip.
I did what one man could do to relieve
the unfortunate, establishing a health de-
partment for Palestine, and soup-kitchens

in Jerusalem at which 330 people are fed daily.

"Jerusalem stands on a hill, and there is every reason why it should be made as healthful and delightful a place to live as the most modern city of the world. What is chiefly needed is modern water-works. There is plenty of water to be had if proper pumping stations were erected. At the present time water is the most precious possession of the household. It is kept in cisterns under lock and key; every drop of it is valuable, because there is no water system available. The defects of the sanitary arrangements of the city on this account are terrible.

"In Jerusalem there is only one good hotel, and what capital is invested there is mostly foreign. There is some rumor that a trolley-line is to be built from Jerusalem to Jaffa, which is being financed, I believe, by Belgian capital. There is absolutely no American money invested anywhere in

Palestine, and yet there should be, because the country is fruitful. I have seen no better orange groves anywhere than in Palestine, and, besides, the world owes a tribute to the historic features of the Holy Land."

While in Jerusalem a few years ago looking upon the great needs of the people, I could but long that some intelligent, aggressive, and wealthy American Hebrew might be moved to become personally interested in the city and do the very work that Mr. Straus now proposes to do. The breaking of the power of Turkey makes these improvements a possibility. The time of the Gentiles is almost ended. It will not be long until Turkey's power in Palestine will be entirely destroyed, and then progress will go forward rapidly. Wealthy Jews will go back to Jerusalem and all the appliances of modern science will be called into requisition to make it a healthful and beautiful city. As for the

means which God may use in the fulfillment of His promise of course no one is
able to positively predict, but that God
will keep His word there is no question,
and our hearts rejoice as we see the fulfillment of prophecy—the improvement of
Jerusalem and the restoration of the Jews.

"And the seventh angel sounded; and there were great voices in heaven, saying, The kingdoms of this world are become the kingdoms of our Lord and His Christ; and He shall reign for ever and ever."

CHAPTER VII.

THE SPREAD OF THE GOSPEL.

In the closing chapters of the gospel of Matthew, our Lord Jesus has much to say with reference to His second coming. In the 24th chapter and 14th verse He says, "And this gospel of the kingdom shall be preached in all the world for a witness unto all nations; and then shall the end come."

The reader will notice that our Lord does not say this gospel shall be preached until all the world is brought to repentance and saving faith, but He says it is to be preached for a witness. Men shall finally be judged in the light of the truth which was preached to them and rejected by them.

The outlook for the rapid spread of the gospel is most hopeful. Notwithstanding the unbelief and backsliding with which we are surrounded, the faithful people of the Lord are stirred up on the subject of foreign missions as never before in the history of the church, and the entire heathen world is open to receive the gospel.

That motto, "The evangelization of the world in this generation," was born of a genuine Christian zeal and faith. The Laymen's Movement, The Students' Volunteer Movement and all of these great missionary movements is the movement of the Holy Spirit upon the true disciples of the Lord to make haste in carrying the gospel to the ends of the world.

The past few years have seen the most marvelous turning to God among heathen peoples ever witnessed in Christian history. Perhaps the missionary enterprise and success now going forward in Korea is without a parallel. All India shot through with western civilization under the influence of the British empire, lies open to the blessed influences of the gospel and is responding to Christian evangelism in so marvelous a manner that many thousands of them are clamoring for Christian baptism, while missionaries cannot be hurried to the field rapidly enough to supply these new converts with spiritual teachers.

The awakening of China and her rapid progress and outstretched hand for the sympathy and help from Christian nations is one of the marvels of the ages. Africa is begging for the bread of life, and missionaries traveling through the dark continent are received with gratitude and followed with entreaty to remain and teach and train the people in the things of the gospel of Jesus Christ.

We doubt not that the next few decades will see the giving of more money, the sending of more missionaries, and more widespread and blessed results in all the great fields than has been experienced within the past hundred years; it is not unreasonable to hope that within this generation the gospel will have been carried to the utmost bounds of the earth, and that every human habitation in desert waste and jungle, in mud hut and up among the tree dwellers, will have heard that Jesus Christ by the grace of God hath tasted death for every man; that His precious blood cleanseth from all sin, and that He is coming back to set up His kingdom in the world to reign and rule in glory over His redeemed people.

It would seem there could be no greater stimulus to missionary zeal and enterprise than the glorious thought that when this gospel is preached to all the world, "Then shall the end come." The end of Satan's reign, the awful waste and ruin of war, the whisky traffic, the white slave trade, starvation, plague and pestilence and the waste and wreck and ruin of human life; and the introduction of a golden age in which Satan shall be bound and cast into the pit, and Jesus Christ shall reign over and rule the earth and the prayer which He taught us from His own blessed lips, and has been offered by the multitudes of Christians through the ages, shall be answered and realized in our earth: "Thy kingdom come, Thy will be done in earth, as it is in heaven."

Believers in the premillennial coming of Christ are accused of being "star gazers." It is said that they are more given to looking up for the coming of the Master than they are to zealous service for the Master. This accusation is evidently false. Our observation is that no class of people is more actively engaged in spreading the gospel and laboring for the salvation of the lost than those whose hearts are stirred and stimulated by the "blessed hope."

Dwight L. Moody was not an idler in the camps of the Lord's hosts, supinely waiting for the coming of the Master, but during his life was one of the most active, earnest, and fruitful evangelists in all the world.   Mr. Torrey, Mr. Chapman, Gypsy Smith, and Billy Sunday are among the most aggressive evangelists in the world today, and they all hold the premillennial view of the coming of our Lord.

Time would fail us to tell of a great host of earnest souls connected with the holiness movement: pastors, evangelists, missionaries, teachers, and devout people scattered throughout the land, and connecting links in a golden chain of faith around the world, who love and labor with sweet expectation that we are very rapidly approaching the close of the present dispensation and the glorious inauguration of the kingdom of peace on earth and good will to men under the reign of the Lord Jesus Christ.

Three of the greatest missionary enterprises in all the world today in their preaching and teaching lay special emphasis upon the second coming of Jesus, and teach the premillennial view, namely: The Taylor

"China Inland Mission," the "Christian Alliance Mission," and "The Oriental Mission."

The intelligent zeal and consecration of the hundreds of missionaries under the influence of these three great organizations challenge the admiration and respect of Christian people everywhere. Tens of thousands of souls are being brought to Christ under their influence, and are being taught to watch and pray and keep their lamps trimmed and burning that they may meet their Lord in peace.

In our recent evangelistic tour around the world we found no more devoted, zealous, and happy missionaries, those who have forsaken home and native land and gone out to carry the gospel to the multitudes in heathen darkness, than those people who are fully persuaded that the "coming of the Lord draweth nigh."

No sweeter thought can stir the human heart than that which thrilled the hearts of

the disciples when they returned from
Mt. Olivet from which Jesus Christ had
ascended, and where they had been assured by the angels who stood by them, as
He went up, that in like manner He would
return again. They returned to Jerusalem with joy, remembering that their sepa-
ration was temporary and that there would
be a blessed reunion of companionship with
their Lord, from whom they should be separated no more.

For a broken-hearted, sinful peni-
tent, to trust in Jesus for mercy, and to obtain His pardoning grace; to learn about
Him in searching the Scriptures, in medita-
tion and prayer, in conflict and struggle, in
all the various and trying experiences of
life, to consecrate to Him entirely and experience the cleansing power of His precious blood, to serve Him with a glad
heart and free, to commune with Him
through the illumination and intercession of
the blessed Spirit, to labor for Him with

a holy love that rejoices to express itself in service, and to wait for His coming with the comfortable hope that it will not be long —this is Christian experience which brings victory over the world, the flesh, and the devil. It makes life worth living, it delivers one from the charm and fascination of the world and sets the affections on things that are eternal.

If the whole Protestant Church could get such a conception and come into such an experience, with what enthusiasm and joy she would bring her offering to the treasuries of the Lord, and give her sons and daughters to carry the gospel to the neglected people of the earth, and how soon there would be no desolate places in the remotest bounds of human habitation that had not heard the good news of saving grace through the atonement of Jesus Christ. There can be no greater protection for the bride against the allurements and fascinations of the world, and no motive more powerful to stir her up to secure her white robes betimes, and keep them unspotted, than that she should be looking with joyful expectation for the coming of her Bridegroom.

The great backslidden and worldly multitudes of professed Christians in the church who are thinking nothing of the white robes of righteousness and who find their enjoyment in mingling with the unregenerated and sinful, have put far away the coming of the Saviour. They do not desire Him, they do not expect Him, they cannot understand those who do, and they belong to those who mock and scoff at the thought of His coming. Not so with those who are saved by His power, filled with His love, and read with glad delight the precious promise with which He closes His last written revelation to His followers: "Surely, I come quickly." With the beloved disciple we exclaim, "Even so, come, Lord Jesus."

Years ago when I was in a state of indecision with reference to the doctrine of entire sanctification, and the possibility of an instantaneous cleansing from the carnal nature through faith in Christ, I had occasion to reflect upon the fact that all of the most wicked and godless elements of society were unfriendly to this great doctrine and experience. That in the very nature of things the frivolous people connected with the modern stage, the selfish people connected with the whiskey traffic, lewd and godless wretches of the underworld, the proud and arrogant classes who live in luxury and seek the gratification of the appetites of the flesh, would be unfriendly to holiness—a pure heart, and a life given to God in genuine consecration and righteousness.

These considerations had a powerful influence upon my mind. It was quite reasonable to suppose that those who love God supremely, who desire His glory, who fully believe in the atonement made by Christ,

in the personality and presence of the Holy
Ghost in the world, ought not and would
not object to the full benefits of the sufferings and death of our blessed Lord; that
if it were possible to be cleansed from all
sin, and made pure through the atoning
merits of Jesus, they would be glad to en-
joy such privileges and enter upon such an
experience.   These reasonings helped me
to determine that my thoughts, desires,
prayers, faith, teachings, and experience by
God's grace, should be out of harmony
with the selfish, wicked, and base elements
of society, and in harmony with the devout
and spiritual people of God

The same process of reasoning will hold
good with reference to the doctrine of the
coming of our Lord.   Our post-millennial
brethren may be sure that any arguments
they may produce in their efforts to prove
that Jesus will not come for thousands of
years, that any sarcasm or ridicule they
may fling at those who long for and expect

Him soon, will be pleasing to, and meet
with the heartiest approbation of the most
wicked and worldly elements in society.
No teaching could bring greater conster-
nation to the liquor traffic, the lewd stage,
the white slave trader, the red-light district,
the riotous rich, the indifferent and godless
multitude, than to be convinced that we are
rapidly approaching and very near the end
of the present dispensation, that in the immediate future the Son of God whom they
have ignored, rejected and blasphemed,
will appear in glory with His mighty angels, taking vengeance upon His enemies.

Let me say in all kindness and Christian
love to our post-millennial brethren, it
would be wise and well to consider these
things seriously, and in the preaching of
their notions and theories postponing the
coming of our Lord to some very indefinite
and distant period thousands of years in the
dim future, to be very careful lest they
grieve the heart of the expectant bride of

the Savior and comfort the hearts of the wicked and dissolute in their sins. The Master has said: that He will come "In an hour that ye think not;" "when eating and drinking, marrying and giving in marriage," they will be neither desiring nor expecting Him; they will be mocking and scoffing at those who are "trimming their lamps" with holy joy; and suddenly, as the lightnings illumine the darkness, the gates of glory will swing open and Christ will come in triumph.

I cannot conceive that the preaching of post-millennial theories could produce conviction for sin, stir the hearts of men to repentance, warn and woo them away from worldliness, and lead them to make haste to robe themselves in the white garments of holiness, and see to it that their vessels are full of oil.

On the other hand it is the experience of preachers and evangelists everywhere, that the earnest preaching of the scriptural doctrine of the coming of the Lord mightily awakens the hearts of men and turns them to repentance, and brings them to speedily seek salvation. This writer has had occasion to notice the gracious effect upon his own Christian experience, and the powerful effect upon the people when he has preached on this great subject, giving the scriptures and pointing out the reasons why he believes that we are rapidly approaching the end of this age, and the inauguration of a glorious dispensation in which Jesus Christ shall reign and rule without a rival throughout all the earth.

"Abstain from all appearance of evil. And the very God of peace sanctify you wholly; and I pray God your whole spirit and soul and body be preserved blameless unto the coming of our Lord Jesus Christ."
·—Paul, I Thes. 5:22, 23.

CHAPTER VIII.

A THOUSAND YEARS FOR A DAY.

In Luke's gospel the 9th chapter and 27th verse, Jesus said to His disciples: "But I tell you of a truth, there be some standing here, which shall not taste of death, till they see the kingdom of God."

This scripture has been very largely misunderstood, some getting the idea that it meant that some one of the disciples should live until the close of the gospel dispensation and the coming of Jesus in His glory, but the following scriptures make plain the meaning of Jesus. "And it came to pass about an eight days after these sayings, He took Peter and John and James, and went up into a mountain to pray. And as He prayed, the fashion of

His countenance was altered, and His raiment was white and glistering. And, behold, there talked with Him two men, which were Moses and Elias: Who appeared in glory, and spake of His decease which He should accomplish at Jerusalem. But Peter and they that were with him were heavy with sleep: and when they were awake, they saw His glory and the two men that stood with Him. And it came to pass, as they departed from Him, Peter said unto Jesus, Master, it is good for us to be here: and let us make three tabernacles; one for Thee, and one for Moses, and one for Elias: not knowing what he said. While he thus spake, there came a cloud, and overshadowed them: and they feared as they entered into the cloud. And there came a voice out of the cloud, saying, This is my beloved Son: hear Him." Luke 9:28-35.

In Peter's second epistle on the coming of the Lord he refers to this transfiguration experience in first chapter, 16, 17 and 18 verses, where he says: "For we have not followed cunningly devised fables, when we made known unto you the power and coming of our Lord Jesus Christ, but were eye-witnesses of His majesty. For He received from God the Father honour and glory, when there came such a voice to Him from the excellent glory, This is my beloved Son, in whom I am well pleased. And this voice which came from heaven we heard, when we were with Him in the holy mount."

These scriptures fully explain the saying of Jesus, that "there be some standing here, which shall not taste of death, till they see the kingdom of God." His transfiguration· and the appearance of two distinguished servants of God with Him on the mount was the coming of the Lord in miniature. Jesus was revealing beforehand to His followers His coming glory, and had with Him on the mount two witnesses of

His grace and power: Moses, who had died and been raised up, representing the resurrection power which will bring the Lord's saints in triumph from their graves when He appears, and Elias, who had never died, but had been translated, representing that great company of Christians who shall be living when Jesus Christ appears, and who will be changed, translated in the twinkling of an eye.

In this same epistle Peter calls attention to the fact that in the last days scoffers will come, walking in their own lusts and saying: "Where is the promise of His coming?" He also mentions the fact that these scoffers have forgotten the judgments of God and how that a previous dispensation has been closed out in the destruction of those who rejected divine mercy. "For," says he, "this they willingly are ignorant of, that by the word of God the heavens were of old, and the earth standing out of water and in the water: Whereby the world that then was being over-flowed with water, perished: But the heavens and the earth, which are now, by the same words are kept in store, reserved unto fire against the day of judgment and perdition of ungodly men." 2 Pet. 3:5-7.

Peter's prophecy that the time would come when men would forget the great fact of the flood has certainly been fulfilled. The multitudes do not remember the flood, or call to mind the fact that God "will not always chide, neither will He keep his anger forever," but that He will punish those who persist in sinning against Him. Many men today, claiming to be religious teachers, deny that there ever was a flood. There are plenty of gospel ministers, who in their conceit take pleasure in proving that such a flood as is described in the Holy Scriptures, is a scientific and physical impossibility. The judgments of God are forgotten and the teachings of His word are set at naught, a marvelous fulfillment of the prophecies of the inspired writers.

In second Peter, 3rd chapter, and 8th verse, we read: "But, beloved, be not ignorant of this one thing, that one day is with the Lord as a thousand years, and a thousand years as one day." There is much more in the Scriptures than will appear upon the surface. To get the meaning of the Spirit, one must search the Scriptures in humility and prayer.

It is the delight of God to hide the precious truth from those who do not desire it; "The secret of the Lord is with them that fear Him." The Scriptures abound in parables, illustrations, and figures. The Lord packs a great depth of meaning into remarkably few words, and delights to reveal to the humble hearts who love Him the unfolding of future beforehand, that they may prepare themselves for things to come.

The millennium—the glorious reign of

Christ is referred to many times in the Bible. The Sabbath day is a beautiful type of the coming age of peace and tranquillity. It was no mere accident that divided the week up into seven days, but infinite wisdom indexed in this division the whole of the probationary period of man. Each day in the week representing a thousand years, and the Sabbath with its rest from toil, its quiet atmosphere, its holy devotions representing the seventh thousand when the week of toil and war and satanic rule shall have passed away and Christ shall have come in His glory.

We had approximately two thousand years before the flood; a like period before the fall of Jerusalem; and now almost two thousand years in which to spread "the gospel of the kingdom." We are rapidly approaching the close of the sixth thousand years of our week of human history. We are late Saturday evening, and time is passing swiftly, events are mustering rapidly,

the twilight of the great apostasy is falling
upon us, and perilous times are gathering
like the hurrying regiments of a mobilizing
army.

The wandering Jews have turned their
faces back toward Palestine and are has-
tening by tens of thousands to the Holy
Land. The evangel of the gospel is
speeding to the ends of the earth with the
message of the love of God, the crucifixion
of Jesus, salvation through His atonement,
and His coming in glory to receive His
bride. The dawn of the great Sabbath
of a thousand years is not far distant.

It is delightful to reflect upon the conditions which will then obtain. There
will be no more war, the earth no longer
drenched with human blood, the sword
will be turned into the pruning hook; the
sweet song bird will build its nest in the
neglected cannon's mouth, and the dawn
of peace will spread her white pinions over
the universal brotherhood of man. There

will be no more whiskey traffic; this demon will be driven to Hades with its father and shut up in the pit and sobriety will reign throughout the earth.

There will be no more plague or destructive earthquake or wasting pestilence or bursting volcanoes annihilating its helpless multitudes, or tidal waves, sweeping doomed cities from the shores of time. The bitter cold will be moderated, the burning heat will be cooled, the earth will be restored and will roll in ethereal light, baptized and blessed with the infinite love of the Father.

Then let us gird ourselves afresh for battle and press the great work of spreading the gospel, waiting with prayer and song until the week of toil is ended and the Sabbath of a thousand years of rest and peace shall break upon our planet, and the Christ who came to earth in humiliation to hang on the cross of shame, shall come back in glory to sit upon the throne of universal empire.

The servants of the Lord have lived in this world with their Master gone away to prepare a place for them, while Satan made fearful ravages among the sheep of His pasture. They long to dwell upon the earth with Satan bound and cast out, and Jesus Christ here reigning in power. We are well aware that there are objectors who suggest that Jesus Christ is too great and holy to live upon this earth. We would remind them that Jesus Christ is the "same yesterday, today, and forever." He was just as holy when He was in this world without where to lay His head, mocked, ridiculed, persecuted, and crucified as He is today.

If Jesus Christ was not too holy to ride into Jerusalem upon an ass' colt, He is not too holy to ride into Jerusalem upon the Shekinah cloud of glory. If He was not too holy to hang upon the cross and die for the race, He is not too holy to sit upon a throne and reign over the race. If He was not too holy to be mocked and ridiculed by the multitudes when He hung on Calvary in humiliation and agony, He is not too holy to be worshiped by the multitudes while He rules in righteousness and truth. This earth is to be redeemed; its believing, obedient people are to be redeemed, and the Lord Jesus is to reign and rule just as supremely here as He reigns and rules in any other part of the universe.

"For this we say unto you by the word of the Lord, that we which are alive and remain unto the coming of the Lord shall not prevent them which are asleep. For the Lord Himself shall descend from heaven with a shout, with the voice of the archangel, and with the trump of God: and the dead in Christ shall rise first: then we which are alive and remain shall be caught up together with them in the clouds, to meet the Lord in the air: and so shall we ever be with the Lord. Wherefore comfort one another with these words."—Paul, I Thes. 4:15-18.

Chapter IX.

MEMORIALS AND PROMISES.

"The practice of the presence of God is the best preventive against sin." To stay the mind on God, to cultivate and carry in the heart and brain thoughts of His presence, almightiness, holiness, and compassion is to elevate the soul into a realm of righteousness and peace. "Thou wilt keep him in perfect peace, whose mind is stayed on Thee." Isa. 26:3.

In the morning of human history God established certain memorials and made certain great promises that were intended to keep the thought of Himself in the minds of the people. The Sabbath Day, the tithe law, the rite of circumcision, the feast of the passover were all intended to be reminders of the divine presence and authority of God in the world, and man's dependence and obligation to a loving obedience, faith, and consecration.

With the introduction of the new dispensation, came in the place of the feast of the Passover the sacrament of the Lord's Supper, and that form of prayer called, "The Lord's Prayer," and the promise of the Lord's return. These memorial institutions of our religion have had a powerful influence upon the Church of God. Ever since the organization of the Church in the old dispensation they have been common centers around which religious life has circled; they have been constant reminders and benedictions to the servants of God.

There is nothing more gracious and powerful in its influence upon people than promises freighted with expectation of great and triumphant events ahead. It was the wisdom of God in the establishing of the Hebrew Church to promise His people a coming Messiah. As prophet after prophet came upon the stage of a~

tion, looking down the dim vista of time, he beheld a coming King. The people listened in wonder and awe while the rapt seers told in words of burning eloquence of the unparalleled power and glory of His reign. "Abraham saw His day and was glad."

Moses said: "The Lord thy God will raise up unto thee a Prophet from the midst of thee, of thy brethren, like unto me; unto Him ye shall hearken." Deut. 18:15.

Daniel said: "And in the days of these kings shall the God of heaven set up a kingdom, which shall never be destroyed: and the kingdom shall not be left to other people but it shall break in pieces and consume all these kingdoms, and it shall stand forever." Dan. 2:44.

Seven hundred years before the Judean shepherds were startled in their midnight watches by the song of the angels, announcing the birth of the world's Redeemer, the prophet Micah had pointed out the country and named the village where Jesus Christ was to be born. "But thou, Bethlehem of Ephratah, though thou be little among the thousands of Judah, yet out of thee shall He come forth unto me that is to be ruler in Israel." Micah 5:2.

These prophecies, with many others equally definite, kept devout people throughout Hebrew history on the tiptoe of desire and expectation for their coming Messiah. There was nothing that had so powerful an influence upon the Hebrew people as this promise; in it was centered the meaning of ceremony and sacrifice. It was the greatest event that loomed in their future, bound them together, with hope and prayer and longing.

When the new dispensation was inaugurated the Church was again to be stimulated, infused, and blessed with the promise of the coming Christ. Jesus made these promises to the disciples. The angels brought these promises when the Lord ascended, the apostles wrote them in their epistles, and they have been the hope of the church throughout the long weary centuries; they are being read afresh now by multitudes of believers as never before in Christian history, and we believe that the signs of the times all point to the sudden appearance of our Lord. that from this time the events of history will move forward upon the double-quick until prophecy is fulfilled, Satan is bound, Jesus descends, the sainted dead are raised, and there will be inaugurated a reign of peace and righteousness in which the glorious prophecy concerning the Kingdom of heaven will be fulfilled in every part.

"And the Lord make you to increase and abound in love one toward another, and toward all men, even as we do toward you: to the end He may stablish your hearts unblameable in holiness before God, even our Father, at the coming of our Lord Jesus Christ with all His saints."—Paul, I Thes. 3:12, 13.

CHAPTER X.

THE SECOND JOHN THE BAP-
TIST.

When Jesus came into the world the
first time, John the Baptist came as His fore-
runner, preparing the way with his earnest,
rugged ministry, and stirring up the hearts
and expectations of the people with great
eagerness for the coming of the Lord.
When Jesus comes the second time, no
doubt a John the Baptist will come before
Him, preparing the people to receive Him.
We believe that John the Baptist is here
now, and that John the Baptist is the great
modern Holiness Movement which, in
some form, is found in all the Christian
world, and in every great mission field.

The Holy Spirit is stirring a multitude
of pastors, evangelists, and teachers to
mightily call upon the people to seek holiness, to be cleansed from all sin, to be

filled with the Spirit, to put on the white robes of sanctification—the wedding garment—and be ready and watching for the appearing of the blessed Christ. The Spirit is especially impressing the servants of the Lord to appeal with great earnestness to God's children to seek a full and complete deliverance from all sin, and to keep their garments unspotted from the world.

This movement is not by any means confined to the followers of John Wesley, but it has touched all religious denominations. "The Christian Alliance," "The Keswick Movement," and other religious movements are laying great stress upon full redemption from sin and the coming of the Lord.

The writings of the apostles connected very closely these two great truths—purity of heart, white robes, wedding garments and the coming Bridegroom. To us this very widespread cry of the Church of God among all denominations and in all countries, coupling these two Bible teachings together—heart purity and the coming of Jesus—white robes for the bride and the coming of the Bridegroom, is quite significant.

We would suggest to the reader that whatever the facts may be in the case, there is no place for ridicule for the injunction of Christ and the inspired writers was that we should watch, keep our lamps trimmed and burning, and be always ready and looking with joyful hopefulness for the appearing of the Lord Jesus.

Such an attitude of soul is one of the best possible safeguards against immersion in worldliness, or undue love of material things which leads to forgetfulness of God and indifference to the things of salvation. There can be no greater stimulus to holiness and to unselfish and zealous service, than to be always comforting the heart with the thought that "the coming of the Lord draweth nigh."

"The wolf also shall dwell with the lamb, and the leopard shall lie down with the kid; and the calf and the young lion and the fatling together; and a little child shall lead them. And the cow and the bear shall feed; their young ones shall lie down together: and the lion shall eat straw like the ox, and the sucking child shall play on the hole of the asp, and the weaned child shall put his hand on the cockatrice' den. They shall not hurt nor destroy in all my holy mountain: for the earth shall be full of the knowledge of the Lord as the waters cover the sea."—Isa. 11:6-9.

CHAPTER XI.

THE MILLENNIUM.

The word Millennium means a thousand years. When used with reference to the second coming of Christ it refers to the thousand years of His personal reign upon the earth.

There is a widespread and unscriptural teaching among men that at the second coming of Christ He will immediately set up the final judgment. A careful investigation of the subject in the light of God's Word reveals the fact that the coming of Christ, the resurrection of the holy dead, and the translation of believing saints, on earth at the time of His appearing, and the general Judgment Day are different and distinct events and are separated from each other by more than a thousand years.

When Jesus comes to set up His millennial reign, Satan will be bound, cast into the pit, and remain there during the millennial period.

During this period Christ shall reign in great glory and peace over the resurrected and translated saints. The unholy dead will not be resurrected at the second coming of the Lord. The scripture teaching is very definite and clear on this subject. "And I saw thrones, and they sat upon them, and judgment was given unto them: and I saw the souls of them that were beheaded for the witness of Jesus, and for the word of God, and which had not worshipped the beast, neither his image, neither had received his mark upon their foreheads, or in their hands; and they lived and reigned with Christ a thousand years. But the rest of the dead lived not again until the thousand years were finished. This is the first resurrection. Blessed and holy is he that hath part in the first resurrection: on such the second death hath no power, but they shall be priests of God and of Christ, and shall reign with Him a thousand years." Revelation 20:4-6.

There are many references to the first resurrection and the gracious reign of Christ found in the Scriptures. In Phil. 3: 11, in revised version, Paul said: "If by any means I might attain unto the resurrection *from* the dead." In 1 Corinthians 15:22 we read, "For as in Adam all die, even so in Christ shall all be made alive. But every man in his own order; Christ the first fruit; afterward they that are Christ's at His coming."

This scripture does not mean to teach that when Christ appears all the dead will be resurrected, but that they that *are Christ's* will be resurrected. In Luke 14:14 we read: "And thou shalt be blessed: for they cannot recompense thee: for thou shalt be recompensed at the *resurrection of the just.*"

There is to be a short period of time be-

tween the close of the thousand years' reign
of Christ and the general judgment. This
fact is very definitely stated in Rev. 20:7-
10. "And when the thousand years
are expired, Satan shall be loosed out of
his prison, and shall go out to deceive the
nations which are in the four quarters of the
earth, Gog and Magog, to gather them together to battle: the number of whom is as
the sand of the sea. And they went up on
the breadth of the earth, and compassed the
camp of the saints about, and the beloved
city: and fire came down from God out of
heaven, and devoured them. And the devil that deceived them was cast into the lake
of fire and brimstone, where the beast and
the false prophet are, and shall be torment-
ed day and night forever and ever."

There are three great future events spoken of very definitely and clearly in this remarkable 20th chapter of the book of Revelation. First, the coming of Christ, binding and casting out of Satan, and the thou-

sand years of Christ's reign. Second, the loosing of Satan from his prison, the apostasy and deceiving of the nations, closing out with the great battle and the casting of Satan into the pit to remain there in torment forever and ever. And third, the final judgment, graphically described in the following verses: "And I saw a great white throne, and Him that sat on it, from whose face the earth and heaven fled away; and there was found no place for them. And I saw the dead, small and great, stand before God; and the books were opened: and another book was opened, which is the book of life: and the dead were judged out of those things which were written in the books, according to their works. And the sea gave up the dead which were in it; and death and hell delivered up the dead which were in them; and they were judged every man according to their works. And death and hell were cast into the lake of fire. This is the second death. And whosoever

was not found written in the book of life
was cast into the lake of fire." Rev. 20:11-
15.

We are well aware that there are those
who are quite inclined to eliminate this remarkable chapter in the book of Revelation
from this discussion.   They are disposed to
question its authority.   They talk about its
standing alone without corroboration in the
general teaching of the Bible.   We have
no sympathy with this criticism, but ac-
cept it absolutely at its face value and believe it without a moment's hesitation.

We call the reader's attention to the fact
that this book is safe-guarded against critics and objectors in a most remarkable
way.   In its introduction in the first chapter and third verse, we have the inspired
writer saying: "Blessed is he that readeth,
and they that hear the words of this prophecy, and keep those things which are
written therein; for the time is at hand."
In the closing chapter we find the inspired

writer in the 18th and 19th verses saying: "For I testify unto every man that heareth the words of the prophecy of this book, If any man shall add unto these things, God shall add unto him the plagues that are written in this book: And if any man shall take away from the words of the book of this prophecy, God shall take away his part out of the book of life, and out of the holy city, and from the things of the holy city, and from the things which are written in this book."

We wish to call the reader's attention to the fact that this warning has reference, not to the Bible as a whole, (although it would be a great sin to tamper with any part of the Word of God) but this warning is with specific reference to *"the prophecy of this book."* The Holy Spirit is safeguarding the book of Revelation and impressing upon us the danger of doing just what many people are doing—setting aside, rejecting, and explaining away the great truths contained in this book.

It would seem that thoughtful and pious men would guard most carefully their criticism of this book of prophecy after such serious warnings.

During the Millennium there will be on the earth a time of great grace and blessing.   The song of the angels will be realized.   There will be "Glory to God in the highest, and on earth peace, good will toward men." Luke 2:14.   Think of an age without war, the devastation, bloodshed, sorrow, and ruin it brings.   During this golden age there will be no war,   "And they" (the nations) "shall beat their to pruninghooks; nation shall not lift up swords into plowshares, and their spears into its sword against nation, neither shall they learn war any more." Micah 4:3; Isa. 2:4.

The whiskey traffic in all of its branches, with all its evil effects will go out of existence.   Sobriety, industry, plenty and generosity will be characteristic of the entire race.   Our earth will be changed, the curses that came with sin will disappear and "instead of the thorn shall come up the fir tree, and instead of the briar shall come up the myrtle tree . . . . The wilderness and the solitary place shall be glad for them; and the desert shall blossom as the rose." Isa. 55:13. Isa. 35:1.

Much of the slavish toil now necessary to subdue the earth and bring forth harvests will be done away and there will be peace and plenty on every hand. Enmity and strife will cease in the animal kingdom, and man and beast will enter into a great treaty of peace and live together in happy harmony.

Isaiah describes the conditions that shall exist in the following beautiful words: "The wolf also shall dwell with the lamb, and the leopard shall lie down with the kid; and the calf and the young lion and the fatling together; and a little child shall lead them. And the cow and the bear shall feed; their young ones shall lie down together: and the lion shall eat straw like the ox.   And the sucking child shall play on the hole of the asp, and the weaned child shall put his hand on the cockatrice' den. They shall not hurt nor destroy in all my holy mountain for the earth shall be full of the knowledge of the Lord, as the waters cover the sea."   Isa. 11:6-9.

Those who cherish "the blessed hope" must not forget "the rapture"—the catching away of the saints to meet the Lord in the air when He shall take His bride to Himself.   This "Rapture" shall occur before the Revelation of the Lord coming in glory to set up His kingdom.

It is during the Rapture, while the holy bride of Christ is caught away, that the great tribulation shall come upon the earth. It is at this time that "two shall be grinding at the mill, one shall be taken and the other left; two shall be engaged in the field, one shall be taken and the other left; two shall be sleeping in the same bed, one shall be taken and the other left." It is with reference to the Rapture that the apostle Paul says: "Then we which are alive and remain shall be caught up together with them in the clouds, to meet the Lord in the air; so shall we ever be with the Lord."

The period between the Rapture—the catching away of the saints, and the revelation of the Lord coming with His saints and angels in great glory, is supposed to be a comparatively short period. It is during this period that a wicked and sinful world that has rejected Jesus Christ will have its way with itself and plunge into a depth of anarchy and sin unparalleled in history, and the earth shall be swept with the besom of great tribulation.

The Lord pledges His bride that she shall be delivered from this time of tribulation in these words: "Because thou hast kept the words of my patience, I also will keep thee from the hour of temptation, which shall come upon all the world, to try

them that dwell upon the earth." Rev.
3:10. "Watch ye therefore, and pray
always, that ye may be accounted worthy
to escape all these things that shall come to
pass, and to stand before the Son of man."
Luke 21:36.

How long the period will be between
the Rapture—the catching away of the
saints, and the coming of the Lord in His
glory, no one can tell, hence the great im-
portance of the bride being always ready
for the coming of the Bridegroom.

The last words of our blessed Savior
contained in the closing book of the New
Testament Scriptures give tremendous emphasis to all He said on the subject of His
return to the earth: *"Surely I come quickly."* Let us join our prayers with the beloved John and say: *"Even so, come, Lord
Jesus."* Amen.